Sincerely, Her

Ebony J. Williams

Welcome to your journey to becoming HER

Williams

Sincerely, Her

Copyright © 2018 by Ebony J. Williams

DEDICATION

This book is dedicated to every properly positioned woman waiting for the man she was created for. May you one day be sown back into his side——where you were cut from while he slept.

To my future priestly king, thank you for existing. The mere fact that I know you are somewhere searching the heart of God for me brings me peace and hope. While I cannot say that every day without you is easy, I am fully convinced that every day we prepare for one another is worth the wait.

I look forward to reading over the contents of my heart, which I've spilled out on paper. It is with exceeding joy that I embrace the grace of what is, while smiling at the days of what was.

ACKNOWLEDGMENTS

I want to first thank the Father, Son and Holy Spirit for keeping me, even when I didn't realize I was not trying to be kept. I am so grateful to the Almighty, for the investment and the measure of his anointing that he has given me for his service. I know outside of the Father that I am merely dust and dirt, but he sees something in me and for that, I am eternally humbled.

To my husband Bryan-Thank you for striving daily to be every page of this book. I am grateful for your love, laughter, covering and partnership. Thank you for spending time, searching the heart of God for me. Your presence really does make the difference.

Thank you to my children Essence and Douglas Chandler. They have been my greatest supporters and life editors that keep me on my post. I made a promise to God that if he kept me, I would keep them. And, when I have wanted to get off my post, I consider how they have watched my walk and I am compelled to stay on task to be their example of Father's heart on Earth. And thank you to my wonderful four bonus children who came as a result of marriage. Thank you so much for sharing your father with me. I absolutely love being a part of the family.

A huge thank you to my Mother, Overseer Freda Thorpe for being the textbook version of Proverbs 31. Any mistakes in life I made were never because of her lack of love, guidance, and example. Every woman should be so blessed to sit at the feet of such a tangible example of Kingdom virtue.

INTRODUCTION

My desire to be soft is what birthed this book. The more I wrote, the softer and pliable I became. I pray that something found in these pages, gives you the permission you have been quietly seeking. Permission to heal, permission to prepare, and most importantly permission to embrace your place as his help.

My prayer for the women who read this, is that you experience first the love, light, and hope of Yahweh. His love allows us to be whole enough to position ourselves where we can catch, carry, and handle that which is sent your way with the most fragile touch. Know that no matter how strong we are as women, we were still meant to be soft.

As you choose true love, God's love will drive away the darkness that seeks you out.

Don't ever allow hurt people with holes where their soul use to be, circumstances, or life to tell you that love hurts. The truth is loving people who don't love God, loving people who are selfish, and loving people who are broken–that hurts.

Love builds even the most broken of people. It mends fences and frees those who are prisoners sentenced to death. Love is magical, and it is worth every dream deferred before it. Love is what births new ideas and what sustains even the most dying of gardens. Love that is true and is blended with purpose, is life changing——it is honorable and healing.

Love is not as complicated as people think, nor is it to be taken lightly. Anyone looking for a perfect mate is looking for a lonely life. Every woman wants a superman, but most are too judgmental to love his Clark Kent. Superman wears the cape and saves the day, but Clark Kent is the fragile, flawed and sometimes not-so-together counterpart.

Women oftentimes search so hard for Superman, that they miss an opportunity to grow with Clark. They forget that Clark is who he is all the time, and Superman is who he is only for a few hours. Clark belongs to you, while Superman seems to belong to everyone. The depiction of Clark Kent is indicative of diverse types of men, and not the actual fictional television character. Clark may be different for everyone. For some, he's a porn addict. For some, Clark is an unemployed writer. For yet another group, Clark is simply a Mr. Can't Get Right.

We have to quit looking for Superman. Wear your own cape, and save your own day. Look for a Clark—— a regular guy, with real issues, who you can give a real love. Don't look for a perfected specimen, nor a science project. Look for someone regular, who is fully committed first to the Lord and his purpose, who you can commit to, stand with, love on, pray for, and grow with. When a man has found his place in his purpose and his creator, despite his proclivities- he is unable to be stopped. A whole man who is lead by the Lord, will be happy to transform into Superman for you when necessary, when he knows you honor his presence and not just his performance.

If your Clark happens to struggle a little more than your neighbor's Clark Kent, that's okay, because in being committed to your Clark, you are committed to his journey, his destiny, and his downfalls. I firmly believe that your love, blended with the love of God, along with your future priest's determination, understanding of his own purpose and work——you will make it.

The truth of love is that it is patient. Love is kind. It is integral. It is full of hope and grace (*see* 1Corinthians 13:4-7). Love that is breathed through the lungs of the Father and inhaled through nostrils of prayer and purpose—that love is beautiful.

Sincerely,
Her

WE ARE THE HANDIWORK OF GOD. She shall be called woman is what was said. When he created the woman, he did so with purpose. We are necessary——uniquely, necessarily, different, and here is why.

"She is more precious than rubies; nothing you desire can compare with her. Long life is in her right hand; in her left hand are riches and honor. Her ways are pleasant ways, and all her paths are peace. She is a tree of life to those who take hold of her; those who hold her fast will be blessed." (Proverbs 3:15-18 NIV)

"She selects wool and flax and works with eager hands. She is like the merchant ships, bringing her food from afar. She gets up while it is still night; she provides food for her family and portions for her female servants. She considers a field and buys it; out of her earnings she plants a vineyard. She sets about her work vigorously; her arms are strong for her tasks. She sees that her trading is profitable, and her lamp does not go out at night." (Proverbs 31: 13-18 NIV)

"While the king was at his table, my perfume spread its fragrance. My beloved is to me a sachet of myrrh resting between my breasts. My beloved is to me a cluster of henna blossoms from the vineyards of En Gedi. [**He**] How beautiful you are, my darling! Oh, how beautiful! Your eyes are doves. [**She**] How handsome you are, my beloved! Oh, how charming! And our bed is verdant." (Song of Solomon 1:12-16 NIV)

Historically, the role of a woman in the life of her

husband is so vital, that when God created Adam, he understood that help was needed. I believe that if God wanted to, he could have given Adam a brother or a father, or even just another male friend to walk with Adam, if indeed company was all he needed. Instead he put Adam to sleep and pulled Eve from his side, signifying that she was a part of him. Therefore, only she could minister to and understand him in ways a friend, father, or brother couldn't.

A man can spend all weekend with his friends, and still come home looking for something special in his wife because she possesses his rib. When a husband speaks to his ordained wife, there is something that clicks in her spirit because he is really talking to an extension of himself.

***

When today's women consider females of the Bible to emulate, they consider Esther or Sarah, or even Ruth and Naomi. However, there is one who seems overlooked by most——Abagail (*see* 1Samuel 25).

Abagail was the wife of a man named Nabal who was a drunk. His behaviors made him an enemy to David, and he was about to be killed. When Abagail was made aware of his fate, she set out to meet David, who was on his way to take the life of her husband. She pleaded with David, offered him the word of the Lord, and intercepted the deadly fate of her husband. Nabal's life was spared, and he hadn't even been aware that he was destined to lose it.

That is a wonderful depiction of how a woman's heart concerning the man she loves can also be his saving grace that goes between him and the heart of the Lord. It was the purity and the passion in Abagail that spared her beloved, and that same passion is what moves the heart of God today. Your name may not be Abagail, but you have the same ability to cover and propel your priestly king into his safe place in God. Nabal lost his life soon after, but there was still power in knowing that it was not at the hands of David.

Nabal didn't get the opportunity to show his appreciation, and men may not always articulate it, but the love and protection from his help-meet makes more than a little difference in his life. Never believe that your role in the life of a man, is a small and insignificant one.

Men are branded as the strong ones, but a properly positioned woman (One who has been given to a man by the Lord) can prove that she carries the inner strength necessary to push him and his purpose forward. He has to first already be in forward and strategic motion when she meets him. Her prayers and presence, fan the already burning flame. Stay pure, purposed, and prayerful; then watch the final manifestation of power along the way.

Origin

"So, the Lord God caused the man to fall into a deep sleep; and while he was sleeping, he took one of the man's ribs[a] and then closed up the place with flesh. Then the Lord God made a woman from the rib[b] he had taken out of the man, and he brought her to the man. The man said, "This is now bone of my bones and flesh of my flesh; she shall be called woman, for she was taken from out of man." That is why a man leaves his father and mother and is united to his wife, and they become one flesh."
(Genesis   2:21-24)

The idea that the woman was cut from the man, came from the Lord, himself. And because of that, we understand that covenant is close to the heart of the Lord- He planned It on purpose! There really is an art to being found and courted. The bible never said that Eve frantically went searching the garden for this Adam because she believed he was her beloved. It does not even say that Adam, who was given dominion over the whole garden went searching for Eve. He was content, working the will and direction of the Lord for his life. He had a place to live, a job and a focus. Eve was the Lord's idea for Adam.

So he created someone suitable. There is absolutely nothing wrong with desiring to be found, but following the order keeps the man as the head. When we start out trying to chase and prove, we set a precedent to continue that behavior and we take away a part of Adam's role-his focus. Men chase their dreams and what they see as a treasure.

The part that I love the most was that Adam saw his rib when he woke up. She was there with him when he opened his eyes. That part of the scripture was proof that it takes a man to wake up first to find us-even if we were laying there a part of him all along. Until a man submits to the Lord and finds rest and peace in him, he is unable to find us, and no matter how much we attempt to be found or grab their attention it just will not be time. And when you look at Adam waking up, you can also view it from a standpoint applicable to today, that a man must first wake up to who he is and what his purpose and path is before becoming suitable for his bride. Some times we can be so in a rush to have a husband that we settle for an unprocessed man. And if you know anything about eating something that is not cooked all the way, you understand that it can make you sick.

Just as Adam found Eve when he awakened, so shall you be found. You will be flesh of his flesh and bone of his bone. As I began to write letters to my future priest, that I am going to share with you, I was learning early how to affirm him, but also positioning my prayers, prioritizing my desires and molding healthy expectations. The more I wrote, the more I grew to love him.

Dear Future Husband,

    I can't wait until you find me, my beloved. I don't just want to be your rib; I long to be your peace and the hiding place for your deepest aspirations that you have yet to know exist. I promise to ask God to instill in me a love that will change your life. Each day I prepare my spirit and my heart to sing a song written for only you.

    I will love, honor, cherish, and trust you as you lead our family, because I know you will be led by God first. I will be your wife, best friend, confidant, lover, prayer warrior, chick on the side, ace, spades partner, and mother to our children all wrapped in one. I will be that so that you won't need anyone else. You can trust me with your heart and I ask that you impregnate me with your dreams and visions so that my spiritual womb can birth them. I'm already praying for you daily and understand the need for my covering to be covered also. I am waiting as I seek Father's heart concerning you.

Sincerely,

Her

Dear Future Husband,

I would love to say that I will never upset you, but the truth is we are flesh, and with that disappointments comes. I do however vow that not one sunrise will come, that I will not love you passionately and intentionally.

I understand losses, and because of them I value wins. I'm committed to consistently winning with you and not just beside you. Every day I find new ways to fix me; so that I become a better version of myself—— not only for God but for the sake of our journey. I am continuing to purify myself through Christ now, so that I can love you sweetly and with grace and light when you arrive.

Just like in basketball when I would grab the rebound, drop low, and move my elbows to clear space for me to move—allowing no opposing players to be close; it is with that same vigor that I continue to clear space in my soul, so that no one else can get close. I may not know your face, but I know your spirit, and I am grateful that you are the most integral, outstanding, God-honoring, wife-adoring, spirit lead man of integrity and valor.

Thank you for your love and your prayers. They cover me even when I am unaware I am not clothed. You don't complete me, because only God can do that. I am however fully convinced that your love will strengthen me, and smooth out the rough edges that use to give small cuts to my own heart. Waiting for you has become a blessing because I have never adored a man the way that I already adore you.

Thank you for searching the heart of God for me. Soon your search will be a memory, as I roll over and wake to you watching me sleep. I know that Father would dare not hold us back unless it was to finish the final details in us both.

I love you with the undying and consuming passion of Yahweh.

Sincerely,
Her

Dear Future Husband,

I know there is safety in both the natural and the physical with you. As you reach around, holding me close, I clasp the back of your neck gently and you impregnate me with the very vision I will birth for you.

Society has told you that strength is your portion, but always remember that my lap is a safe place for your most vulnerable and private moments. To the world you are a super hero, but to me, you are the most beautiful and precious gift from God——strong and fragile.

As you give me your last name, I will give you a love strong enough to protect you, big enough to feed you, and soft enough to allow you to fall without the fear of you breaking upon landing.

Sincerely,
Her

Dear Future Husband,

One of the things I look forward to the most is standing on one side of the altar with you on the other as we lay hands on the sick and possessed, and drag every demon back to hell——together.

Home will be a place of peace, and ministry will be a place of power. After all, how much more pleased would the Lord be to see the covenant he put together bring the body of Christ back to him one home at a time. As much as I look forward to being taught and lead by you, something stirring hits my intellect when I dream of being loved by you. This love I refer to is not the one that curls my toes, but the love that changes my life.

It causes me to be an even better, more holy, God-honoring, and intensely purified picture, vividly painted on a priceless canvas. This love originates from a blue print that was never used before, and that will be locked in a glass case after because it belongs to only us.

Thank you for provoking me to be an even more glorious and breathtaking version of myself.

Sincerely,

Her

LOVE NOTE:

We lost our way on the journey. We didn't feel safe enough to be unguarded, and were too soft-so we thought, to be respected. Father and mother issues, battles with self-image, and not forgetting the times that we have given to others more than we have received, has caused a rather tainted imagery.

Instead of being unappreciated, we vowed to stay on lock. Releasing our femininity——the very essence of what a man needs to feel safe, we choose for it to not be an option. We place bricks around our heart, and before we knew it, we forgot that we were made to be the weaker vessel (see 1 Peter 3:7). Men were made to be needed, which isn't the same as worshipped.

Because we refuse to be hurt again, we forget that the defensive posture we take could rob the very one who desires to simply love us, of the opportunity to love us as Christ loves the Church (see Ephesians 5:25). Inner healing is vital to healthy love giving. The lack of it could cause him the very pain we ourselves have refused to be wrapped in.

The pain of what happened to you is very real, but so is God, and so is his desire to heal every hurting place with his perfect love. When we finally accept his passionate and pure love, we move into a place where we can give something whole to someone else.

PRAYER OF LOVE:

Father, God——today we lift before you the heart of the woman. Thank you for allowing her to be strong yet soft, bold but fragile, broken but purposed, and kind but firm.

We decree today that the heart of the woman will be hidden—buried in your bosom. Father, we declare that only those kings and priests who stay in your face will find us your gem. We declare that they will be willing to be fragile in the hands of the one sent by you to walk with him. We ask that you keep us hidden in the cleft of the rock. May we be set apart as the rib, only fitting in the ribcage of our set priest.

Father, dust us of the residue of our past disappointments, and let them be filled with your joy, your peace, and your hope. Teach us to be the chief intercessor of our homes. Equip us to sow and build and guard the hearts of our family. Quiet our lips when what we say could be "right," but wrong because of our judgmental and impatient tone. Show us how to deal in the same love that we desire from our priestly kings. Thank you for hearing us and for washing us with your truth.

In Jesus' name, Amen.

Evolution

"Her husband trusts her without reserve, and never has reason to regret it. Never spiteful, she trusts him generously all her life long." (Proverbs 31:11-12 MSG)

When many women think about a man trusting her, they first think of trusting what she will or will not do with her body. While that is part of trust, there are things that a man may want from us that mean even more to him. Can he trust her with his deepest goals and desires? She loves his strength and his protection, but what will she do when he hands her his truth? One of the worst infractions against a man who trusts us would be to take what he speaks in private and then run the details of it down to every friend and family member we have.

Unless the man that we love is telling us that he is going to harm someone, there are certain talks that should remain reserved for the pillow. Remember that you will love your mate, but your family and girlfriends are not mandated to. Keep what is precious to him safe, so you don't find yourself having to re-introduce the new and improved him to the people who lost faith because of what they should not know. A man of standard is not drawn to women who find purpose in being the New York Times publication with every moment of her life. Remember a wise woman is always building.

Dear Future Husband,

Each time there is a tough situation ahead of my home, I wonder how you would handle it. I already believe that Father gives you strategy that will shift and cover our existence daily. I am waiting with exceeding joy for the guidance and protection that will only come from you.

Although I have been the problem solver for many years, I already find it easy to trust and rest in your care. I know that trusting a man who is led by our Father leaves me with no liability. Because God is your power source, your strength and vision are focused and dependable.

Thank you for protecting while we are both preparing. Our purpose is worth every moment on my face and every overturned plate for the sake of us.

Sincerely,
Her

Dear Future Husband,

I look forward to your emergence like the night sky awaits sunrise. Somehow, I think you are already preparing to be the priest I need. I am a strong warrior, almost effortlessly at times, but I must admit, the thought of hiding underneath your strength to expose my fragile nakedness sounds more beautiful than any sonnet and more simplistic than any haiku.

Your presence towers over me like the willow tree I sat under on Saturdays in my small country town as a child. I always knew the world was bigger than me, and I always wanted a love with the capacity to encompass my entirety.

Don't tarry much longer. I promise to be every quiet request you made unto the Lord. I will be who your mother prayed you would one day marry. The pictures in magazines that you and your friends skimmed through under the slide as children will not do me justice——I will be more than that.

As I lay here and write this off the top of my soul—no do overs, and no outlines, so shall my love be——natural, beautiful, and free, like the red follicles atop the head that holds my chocolate chip kissed cheeks.

Sincerely,

Her

Dear Future Husband,

I am strong enough to have birthed two children naturally, to have never lost a fist fight, to have climbed trees, and to have went sledding down slate dumps as a child. I am strong enough to lift my weight and then some, to beat the boys in relay races, and to hold my fellow cheerleaders as I threw them up in basket tosses.

I am strong enough to survive rejection, depression, perversion, and the like. My strength is enough to snatch demons and pierce darkness with the light of truth. Yet, I am still soft enough to rub against your soul and feel like satin in your arms. I look forward to being gently loved in your care, because as strong as I am, I am still excited to be your weaker vessel. My strength is for you, and never against you.

Sincerely,
Her

When I positioned myself to start writing letters and even really setting aside time to genuinely pray for my future husband, I found something incredible. I learned that the more you pray for someone and not just about them, your heart begins to change. I slowly went from writing to a phantom person, and just asking the Lord to prosper the work of his hands, to really believing in all of of who he was and who the Lord was fashioning him to be.

The more that I covered all that concerns him, the Lord then began to deal even more with me. I found myself provoked to say," Father whatever would keep me from honoring your son, please reveal it, to heal it, to bless it." I no longer was just praying for my husband; I was being molded into his wife as well. I found myself being more understanding and exercising more patience in all areas. I initially felt like, Okay Lord when will this happen; you said it was coming. That changed into, Father I want him, but I refuse to break him or to have a man who is not yet decided, so take your time healing the both of us.

I remember reconnecting with my now husband ,and him saying that he had never seen me so peaceful or so content with where I was at present. He always knew me to be silly and peaceful, but he could not understand how I seemed like an even better version of the woman he said he always loved. He saw no rush in my spirit for anything except my purpose. When he asked me what happened, all I could say was I had been so wrapped up in my own purpose and children and ministry that I had found peace in Matthew 6:33. When I made the decision to fully make my affections set on pushing what I was given charge over, and simply preparing for what I had been praying for, I found another level of joy.

I did not want anything before its time. And that is my advice to those of you asking the Lord when will you see his hand move for you in the area of your heart. Begin to simply work what is in your hand-be it ministry, career, family or health. There really is no magic wand, or colloquial anecdote for any of it. Make your purpose your priority and prepare for what you are seeking the Lord for. You do not just want to have a husband, you want to be just what he needs in a wife. And one of the best ways to do that is to find yourself and your mission, before you are found and have marriage.

Dear Future Husband,

I feel like I waited my whole life to give you this love. I'm in daily preparation so that what we have will be fireproof and divorce proof. I pray that God would bless the work of your hands, soften your heart, heal your hurts, and put in you a love for me that could only come from Him. We don't need any distractions, so I consistently speak to your past and make sure I cancel every diabolical assignment on your life, even the ones you don't see.

I desire to be your safe place to fall, so I'm learning to give understanding that surpasses even what I knew before. I will cover you in times you are unaware you are naked, and I will never use my tongue to do you harm. I'm keeping my body, so that on our wedding night you would know that you and our destiny was worth the wait.

Only God will come before you, and that includes parents and children, because that is God's design for us. I promise to be your biggest supporter. I'll offer acceptance of all your crazy ideas because in my arms you should be able to dream.

Thank you in advance for being faithful and for being my friend. Our life will be full of passion, patience, purpose, and promise because we will honor God——even while we date and prepare for marriage. There is so much in store for us and I'm blessing God already as if you are here now. It won't be long and before I know it we will share life, love, laughs, and longevity. See you soon!

Sincerely,
Her

LOVE NOTE:

We can be an excellent wife and never come close to being his "help." The choice a man makes in a woman, can be the difference in him working construction, versus him owning the billion-dollar construction company. Although a man who works is honorable no matter the position, there is a different satisfaction that comes from being in the place of power versus working for the one with the power.

The womb can either birth vision or venom. When birthing spiritual babies with defects, it is not always the "sperm," that is defective. The "baby" may have gotten sick while being carried by us. Before asking for a husband, you must understand the rules of being his rib.

A man may never acknowledge his gratitude for it, but he needs your prayers. Even when they are not always the man you pictured, God desires us to cover them as if they were. It is our prayers that may at times convict their heart and change their direction towards paths of destiny that they weren't even thinking about. Please remember that we are never to use our prayers to complain about him to God, but rather lay him out before him.

I have spent many days penning the sentiments of my heart to the man that I love—though I have not met him yet. Here is your chance to do the same. Take the time to write your own letter to your future husband. Be open, and let your heart and pen speak.

Dear Future Husband,

_____

_____

_____

_____

_____

_____

_____

Goodness

"For it is better to live on a corner of the rooftop, than share a house with a contentious woman." (Proverbs 21:19 NIV)

Dear Future Husband,

I have never been one who was good at making empty promises. I vowed to always stay silent before I utter meaningless statements for the sake of being heard. I already take immense joy in the manifestation of every promise I've made to you, our children, and our destiny. I promise to always be the first to hear you, even when you don't feel safe enough to speak yet.

I promise to be the one who will only reject the lies you tell yourself and never reject the lips they came from. I promise to honor you fully, even in a society draped in the garments of dishonorable mentions. I promise to always be your help, even when you forgot that in Abba every hard place can be "hoped." I promise to speak well of you in the public, and protect you in my prayers from what men may curse you with in private.

Beloved, I promise to always keep my body together and strong, so that in our bed chambers I can be the only thing that makes your knees weak. I promise to be solid, because of Christ the solid rock I stand, and we know other ground is sinking sand. I promise to keep honor always in your last name because honor starts at home. In a world full of broken toys and misplaced blocks, I promise to never play with what is precious, and never break what is fragile——your heart. Today I promise and tomorrow I will do it all again, because there were too many yesterdays without you.

My grasp will never slip even when life slopes. I

love you today as if I already knew you once upon a time. I look forward to our lives in happily ever after.

Sincerely,

Her

Dear Future Husband,

Each day that we learn each other, even while waiting for one another, I am moved to operate in love even the more. I am learning new ways to give you respect, and to never cause you to feel unloved or undervalued. While no one is perfect, I am thankful because I know that Father will, and is, placing in you all the tools it will take to love me as he desires.

Sometimes I smile for no reason, because I am confident that each day with you will be worth more than the seemingly millions of days before you. This journey continues to project grace, light, and of hope in our tomorrow——even when today seems shaky. Thank you in advance for being the very thing I prayed for, and the very one that my parents hoped I would be found by, as they sat at the bottom of my covered feet, reading fairytales to me before bed.

I will speak to you in love and I will intentionally listen for your response, not so that I can be right, but so that we can be whole. The thought of winning with you, makes every loss even more sweet.

Sincerely,
Her

Dear Future Husband,

Beloved——it's me again. I want to say that the journey to being found by you is easy, but honestly, it is full of difficulty. The difficulty is not in the waiting——I'd wait 100 years to feel the kiss of my king upon my forehead. No! The hard part is knowing that someone so amazing and so created for me has to exist without holding my hand as they journey down the winding roads of life.

Fear not though, I cover you more than I cover myself because I believe that you are in return covering me the same. Together through Christ, even while apart, I know that our bond is growing roots that will come into full bloom at the divine time.

I love you now, and I will honor and adore you soon. You may not be my God but I will honor you as my head. I will submit to you as my king. I will cover you as I do all things precious, and I will wait for you as I wait for the dawn of each new day. Soon my king and priest...soon!

Sincerely,
Her

Dear Future Husband,

I intend to make this your posture as often as I can. Your head against my chest is so close that I can feel you breathe when I inhale. My bosom should be a place of pleasure for you, and your place of peace. I promise to never have unrealistic expectations for you that box you in a corner set only for the strongest of men.

You are free to dream, to be great, and to be my priest; but also, to be fragile and transparent. Unlike Delilah, when you lay your head in my lap, it's there that some of your greatest strategies will be imagined. It is through my womb that many of them will be birthed.

I am already your greatest supporter and your biggest fan and soon I will be your glory, the brightest jewel in your crown, your only lover, and your help-meet. I long await the moment I can walk to you and be sown back into the side I was once pulled from. Hurry to me.

Sincerely,
Her

LOVE NOTE:

The truth that seems to be unbelievable for some, is that a man needs the same listening ear of that of a woman. To honor your male counterpart, and to respect him is equally as important to him as it is for you to feel beautiful. Use your words to empower him, because he has an entire world outside of the home that freely tears him down. We should never want to be another battle he has to fight.

Nagging, even if the subject is relevant, is never productive, and in fact can be the chisel that breaks away at his strength. If this is an area of struggle for you, spend some time in prayer to work on this.

Let's be honest with ourselves. No one is here, but just you and I. There may have been an incident or person that demonstrated some actions toward us that we allowed to negatively impact how we saw every man after that. That is called unnecessary baggage. Would you allow a stranger at the airport to pick up your personal luggage and go through it? Of course not, but we do that with the one we love at times if we are not intentional. We ask them to open and unpack baggage that does not belong to them, filled with garments they cannot fit.

As I began my journey to healing after divorce, I decided to become intentional about what I fed myself and what I carried. It started with some daily confessions, and I believe that this is a great place and avenue to practice one. You can custom fit them to your own life and situation, but let's deal with the aforementioned baggage, okay? Find a place by yourself and repeat this out loud :

- I am healthy and whole -lacking nothing
- I will not take anything on my journey that was not sent by the Lord for me
- My future husband is not sent to hurt me, but to cover and love me

- My past has no voice in my present
- I am beautiful and I was created on purpose, because my life matters
- I release every ounce of pain and torment in my mind, because it has no place in my life
- I am worth love and respect and I will only accept those things
- Aside from the Lord, I am worthy of being number one in the life of my future priest.
- I am whole and I am enough, and because I am taking this time to heal myself-,I will only draw other whole people to me.
- I FORGIVE everyone who has hurt or disappointed me. I release them from my soul so that I can be healthy and free. I even forgive myself

PRAYER OF LOVE:

Father, we understand that trusting someone to guide us can be hard, but we do not want to break down what you have sent to give us structure.

Teach us how to win him over with our prayers, patience, and kindness. Give us the words to speak to him in a way that he feels loved and heard, and most importantly, respected. Show us areas in ourselves that could hinder him from feeling validated.

Father when there are situations in the relationship that need correcting, allow us both to hear you first that we can hear one another and move towards a healthy solution.

In Jesus 'name, Amen.

Grace

"She opens her mouth with wisdom, and the teaching of kindness is on her tongue". (Proverbs 31:26 ESV)

I believe that we now live in a society that has taught and portrayed that being kind and gracious makes us weak or foolish. The epidemic of social media videos of twerking , mixed with the reality shows that depict loud and callous women who first choose a certain type of man then refuse to respect that man has watered a generation of women down. Now the very thought of speaking to a man with honor and respect has become like a curse word to some. One thing my now husband said to me was, "I did not marry you because you can do everything a man can do. I married you because I am crazy about all the things I cannot do, that you bring to my life."

There is such power in the femininity of our words as well as our presence. I have learned through many years of marriage as well and offering counseling to singles and couples, that a wise and gracious woman can have anything from her priest she wants, and he never know it was even her idea. No matter how powerful and dominating we as women are in the courtroom, boardroom or even our ministry roles, it is okay to just be soft in the arms of the man the Lord gave to lead us. The trick is to give our hand to the man who is first lead by the Lord. It makes trusting his leading that much more easy and worthwhile. There are times in our homes, that we can be totally right, but in the wrong tone. You will find that the Lord will have a much easier time speaking to and dealing with the flesh of our man, when we don't bruise his spirit. Your voice in his ear carries weight, even when it is soft. You can learn to be firm when needed, while still feminine.

Dear Future Husband,

I pray already, that you have men in your camp that will hold you up and help your knees from buckling when the weight of my love sits atop your soul. It's so important to have likeminded soldiers on your journey, so that you are always supported and encouraged to be the best possible version of yourself.

Anyone can find people to party with and chase women who slide down poles, but I pray daily that the covenant keepers that you walk with are keepers of covenant. It will give me peace to know that when the world preys on you, they will be praying over you.

I hope and pray that when society attempts to discourage you from being the amazing priest that I am sure that you are, that those men in arms, would be positivity and strength needed for the journey. I love you and your protectors——my brothers, already. Soon my Priest.

Sincerely,
Her

Dear Future Husband,

While I cannot say that the journey to you has always been easy, I can graciously say everyday has been worth it. I have never been so confident in a man's ability to both love and lead me as I am with you. It's just an inner peace that grows in me like an unborn blessing being fashioned in my womb for 9 months. While many have tried to grab my attention, it remains evident that the footprints in my soul belong to a pair of shoes custom made for you, and I instantly know that you will walk by my side, and they would walk on my heart.

Please understand that I wait for you like the night sky awaits the dawn of the new day. Right when even the smallest glimmer of light shatters darkness, it is there that hope rests. I know night doesn't last always, so promise me one thing. Don't take too long. I am bursting with the joy of my love and honor that will change your life once you change my name.

Sincerely,
Her

Dear Future Husband,

I found myself wondering what color you preferred when I was getting a mani-pedi yesterday. It was amazing to feel you thinking about me as I thought of you and how I love considering your desires already. More than that, I can't wait to hold your hand for the first time, and kiss your eyelids as you breathe in; knowing when you open your eyes and exhale as if it were a dream, I will still be there.

Daily, I ask Abba to keep people from me who will delay your coming. Why waste time on a decoy when I know I will forever love the prototype by which all amazing men are made from——you. It's almost time. There is so much ministry to be done, so many laughs bottled up, that'll hurt our sides, and so many afternoons fishing on the lake to enjoy.

My king, don't rush to me, but don't wait. I want timing to be all Father's, so that we will never have to be apart again.

Sincerely,
Her

Dear Future Husband,

I wish there were words or even utterances to describe the way I feel for you already. The very anticipation of it all is like nourishment for every starving place in me. When I close my eyes, I can almost hear your voice in my ear. You are strong and wise, but gentle enough to be the balm for what is both hidden and ailing in me.

It is beyond unexplainable to know that I will one day be responsible to carry the seed of your destiny and purpose. I am enthralled at the very thought of my womb giving its first kick to signify strength and power in what we will create. The firm touch of your hand wrapped around my abdomen, which engulfs my heart is a reminder that what we have is so pure, purposed, fragile and fertile. I love you already, sweet soul.

Sincerely,
Her

Confession

- I will be careful to be slow to speak
and quick to hear, because words build life

- I know that a wise woman builds her
 home (Proverbs 14:1) and because I am wise, I will
guard what I speak over myself, my family and
home

- My presence sets the temperature in
my home. I am an atmosphere shifter, and because
of that I will always carry peace

- My husband and children can find safety in
my heart for them and my actions towards them.

- Being graceful does not make me weak, it makes
me a woman who knows my strength is not in my
hands, but in my spirit and in what I carry.

LOVE NOTE:

For many of us women, because we are nurturers——instinctively born to love, we can give our heart rather quickly. If the wind blows too hard on a Tuesday many of us feel we are in love right then. But, to gain the heart of true love, walls, landmines, barbed wire, a fire breathing dragon, and so forth must first be defeated.

Men are hunters by design, so for them to love—genuinely love, he must trust you with all the vulnerability that he spent years burying and protecting in explosives. Just as we are fragile, men are equally as fragile, thus requiring the same gentle care we do. If you have been blessed with the heart of a good man, guard it with your very soul and with prayer.

Women are bred to love. It comes as second nature for the average woman. However, the man, on average is the polar opposite. Remember that the same love and affirmation that women desire is also important to a man. His may vary from yours. It may need to be in the form of honor and respect—but do know, that he is just as in need of it as you.

Here is another chance for you to spill your heart. Take a moment and write another letter to your future husband. Remember to be open, and let your heart and pen speak.

Dear Future Husband,

_____

_____

_____

_____

_____

_____

_____

_____

_____

_____

_____

_____

_____

_____

_____

_____

_____

Sincerely,
   Her

Patience

"He makes everything beautiful in its time. He has also set eternity in the human heart; yet no one can fathom what God has done from beginning to end " (Eccl 4:11)

Have you ever rushed out of the house and got to the airport or another destination and realized you had forgotten something of great importance? No? What about baked a sweet treat and when it was finished you could tell you had left the eggs out of the recipe ? You were so in a rush to get something accomplished that you left out or forgot steps that were vital to the finished product.   It bothers you to your core when it happens surrounding a task. What about when you rush and forget something vital that now negatively impacts your purpose.

It is not always that other people play a hand in our own demise. Some times it is a result of lack of time and preparation. During the space of time that you are preparing to be found, put intimate and intentional effort pouring into yourself. The best time to heal and to determine what you   need even from a future mate is before you ever meet them. How can a wonderful man know how to love and show us appreciation if we have not yet determined what those things look like, first.

While it may take sometime to be found, you plan to spend the rest of forever enjoying his love-slow down and focus on the details. What do you need? What causes your greatest smile? What are your deepest fears? What about you could harm your man or bruise his emotions? Those are all important pieces of your laundry that have to be sorted before they can be folded and put into the correct closet and drawers.

As fiercely incredible as we are, there is someone somewhere who is tired of someone else who is just as incredible. It takes more than beauty to build a home. What other elements can you offer to help lay the brick and stone of your covenant? What have you done individually that will both bless and break the unit of marriage? Those are all areas to address before purchasing the dress. This is a long distance race toward eternity, not a sprint.

Determining not just what value a perspective mate has, but also what value we bring to the union is just as important. The purpose of marriage is always to given the Kingdom glory. What role do you play in the glory and beautification? What have to spent time doing in the off season , that will be beneficial when it is time for the team to hit the field? Work on your purpose, posture, presence and your pretty before you meet your partner. When your beauty changes and ages, what have you built that will remain fruitful and in bloom?

PRAYER OF LOVE:

Father thank you for every gift and talent that you have given to me. Thank you for my genuine desire to love your son with every beautiful and pure place in my heart and spirit. While I continue to prepare myself, give me grace to not rush your hand and miss your time by getting out of your will. Thank you for creating a passion in me to first serve you and your plan for my life, then to be intentional about serving my family as you designed. Daily I am committing my desires and my timeline to you, because I trust every bit of me with all of you. Thank you for be a father who cares about what is best for his daughter.

   In Jesus' name , Amen

Trust

"The heart of her husband trusts in her, and he will have no lack of gain. She does him good, and not harm, all the days of her life." (Proverbs 31:11-12 ESV)

Healthy love is a perpetual state of servitude and forgiveness for both men and women. If we are not careful , those two important factors can be overshadowed by our perception of how something should have gone a different way. If we are not careful and persistent in our reach for a pure connection, disappointment can cause us to also be more concerned with making someone feel how we felt versus how they need to.

Have you ever told someone, " I am going to do a you on you." You wanted them to feel the exact way an action of theirs had stung you first. Contrary to popular belief, it may be satisfying in the moment but that is not a healthy reflection of love. Remember that just as Christ has offered us grace for areas he kept hidden from public display, we owe that same grace to our mate. This is not a carte blanche for us to be mistreated, but is does remove space for the enemy to destroy our covenant because our petty spoke louder than our purpose.

As I wrote my future husband letters, and covered him in my prayers, I found new levels of grace for his growth even before his arrival. I continued to remind myself of the areas where I needed a helping hand or a praying and listening heart and ear on my journey. I became specific in what I would speak to Lord about him. I was learning not to leave any details out. I was praying for the impact his childhood had on him. I covered any area that may have been a blind spot in his vision and could cause him to not cover our home as he needed. The best time to cover your husband is long before he ever appears in your life. Allow the Lord to work on him before you ever boggle him down with the list of home repairs and financial obligations in the home.

Always remember that you are precious , but so is the head of your household.

Dear Future Husband,

As I lay here preparing for prayer tonight, I am forced to be thankful for your presence. I feel you even when you are not here. I hear your spirit even in the deepest silence, and I see your love for me lit brightly, even amongst the darkest of night skies.

You are near——I sense you! It is almost time. I feel you as I pray more each day. You were lying next to me in bed the other night. Your presence was the quiet giant that shined the light on the shadowy places that would have tried to consume me as I slept.

Sincerely,
Her

Dear Future Husband,

I cannot wait to wear your ring and give honor to your name, which is already full of integrity. Sometimes I dream about your smile and when I wake, the moon is shining just a little brighter over my bedroom window. I anticipate when the walls of our home are full of laughter and memories we seemingly waited forever to create.

I am already better just because I know you are somewhere looking for me as I wait to be found. I will be a sponge as you pour Kingdom into me. I will understand you because I came from your side. I am aware that when you speak to me, you are literally speaking to a piece of yourself.

As each day draws closer and I continue to prepare; I clear my lap continuously of debris so that you can have a place to rest your head and dream.

Sincerely,
Her

Dear Future Husband,

I believe it starts right here——that moment when our gratitude for what Father has placed between us causes us to fall to our knees in quiet reverence in recognition of his sovereignty. It's amazing how someone I have never met already means the entire world to me.

I'm not longing for our first kiss or even the first time you utter that you love me. The moment that takes my breath away is the very vision of opening my eyes during worship, with tears streaming down my face—— and with lifted hands, I look over and you are just as captivated by the presence of our creator, who thought enough of us to give us both his best. Our worship will be the thread that knits us together right at the chest of the Father, just to the left of his sternum where his heart rests.

Sincerely,
Her

Dear Future Husband,

I prayed for you last night, and you felt so close! I almost reached out to grab your hand. Next to your salvation, I want to be your greatest joy, your warmest smile, and your most meaningful pledge of forever.

My womb anxiously awaits the implantation of your seed of purpose. I want to birth the beginning of a brand-new promise you have never held before.

Soon my king. I can almost smell you——soon!

Sincerely,
Her

LOVE NOTE:

While he thoroughly appreciates when he comes home to a clean home, a warm meal, and your ability to wet his whistle like a professional; a real man of God also wants to know you are in his corner even when he has backed himself into it.

Do you have any prayer power, that you can re-route demonic assignments coming for him? It is hard enough being called by God to love, when as boys they were taught to take things apart with their bare hands. Just give him some time to lay in your lap as you cover him, because what you don't know is there is a world full of women who just want to please him. Dishonor can crack open a door that might end up being the very entrance that darkness uses to creep into your home.

Oftentimes, as women in ministry or any leadership role we find it easier to lead sheep and harder to be led by our priest (husband). It is not because you do not love him, but it is because you were never taught how to balance your divinity and your humanity. Who we lead, deliver, lay out, bring to salvation et cetera, does not remove us of our responsibility to be fragile in the arms of our king.

Our title of Prophet, Apostle, Deaconess, Evangelist, Pastor, and Choir Director does not come before our role of wife, help-meet, boo, baby girl, fox, or sexy to our priest. He does not need a word when we are snuggled up. Sometimes your husband needs prayer, a meal, a giggle, and some "private marital worship" with you. Take your collar and cassock off and just be his 'good thing'. Give him a soft place to land, and he will find it easy to fall.

A woman who loves and is meant for him won't just speak to the king in her man, she will search the innermost parts of his soul to find the scared little boy, and nurture him into his adulthood. Once implanted in her womb, she will take his spiritual and intellectual seed, and birth the nations that through Christ he will govern.

Her ability to cook and clean, keep herself together and even please him physically will keep him coming home, And, her God-ordained grace to push Kingdom with him, and prophesy not just his "next" but live prophetically in his "now," is what will keep him strong in his assignment.

PRAYER OF LOVE:

Father, today give us the words and the posture to be the glory of our husband or future husband. Let us not be the place that causes him strife. Place in us the very love they need from you. Pour it on flesh, that we can be the place they call home and a conduit that brings healing to places they weren't aware were hurting.

Don't allow us to forget that no matter how strong he is, he is not you, and therefore, he will have struggles that we aren't even aware of. Remind us that beauty can fade, but a heart that honors you is a wellspring of life. Thank you for making us so much more than a pretty face. We are your daughters, and that makes us royalty.

In Jesus' name, Amen.

Grit

"Her children rise up call her blessed; Her husband also, and praises her: "Many daughters have done nobly, but you excel them all" (Proverbs 31:28-29 NKJV)

One of the things that I loved the most about the woman we know from scripture as the "Proverbs 31 Virtuous woman," was her posture. The word speaks about her rising early and tending to matters of her home. It did not depict her as a woman who had or offered nothing to her family. It shows her as both resourceful and resilient but also one who was kind and was to be honored and respected by her family. I saw a woman who did not feel that because she did so much for her home, that she had a free ticket to be cold and un-caring. She appeared to have balance in her character.

She could keep her home running like a well oiled machine, but she also was appreciated by her husband and children. Having a plan before having man is important. Men want someone they can build with and who when they are not home, or must travel for business can still cause the operation of the home to flow smoothly without him. While a man wants to be needed, he is not looking for someone who is needy. The difference in the first and second are that one is an asset and the other a liability.

We are the weaker vessel and should be loved gently, but when he hands us something, can we take it and make more? Just as a man gives a womb his seed and it carries and produces a baby, what will we do with any healthy seed given to us?

Dear Future Husband,

   While I look forward to your prayers and your power, I am made to feel like a school girl again when I think about your presence. The thought of slow dancing on the patio under a perfectly lit night sky, even if it's only to the music that resonates quietly from your soul to mine, excites me. In a world that screams loudly to be seen, I am awe-inspiringly in love with the ability to sit in silence and soak in the essence of who you are.

   I'm not simply interested in your humanity. I also look forward to pouring into your divinity. The honor and beauty I have for you, will never make you question again if God loves you. I desire to be his passion for you spilled out in human form. I will never lose faith in the fantasy that you will be my divinely assigned reality. May we be baptized daily in the covenant we call us—— more honest than an all-points bulletin, more satisfying than a wet dream, and more healing than the pool we know as Bethesda. I absolutely love you!

Sincerely,
Her

Dear Future Husband,

Sitting in the Tabernacle waiting for service to begin, one of the greatest smiles comes across my face as I imagine how you would look next to me. Seeing all the families dressed in their absolute best, with faces illuminated with the joy that comes in knowing they are serving God as a unit, makes me more than hopeful; my coals are stoked.

I understand the absolute necessity in standing with you as you stand before our creator to get instructions on how to lead our home. You are my covering, and God is who carries us. I will never take who you are and what you have been appointed to be for granted. You have been one of my most desired heart songs, and the melody of your existence, blended with the harmony of your truth, is proof that all music isn't heard–but the power of it is surely felt.

Sincerely,
Her

Dear Future Husband,

If I close my eyes long enough I can imagine your smell. I picture the light that emits from only your smile, and the touch from your hand on my shoulder just before you wrap me in your arms as I prepare our evening meal.

I anticipate your moments of study, where I can brush pass you just before kissing the back of your head. This is not to disturb your peace, but rather, it is my way to feed and reinforce it. I have prayed for you, and because of that I have revelation into your most deep places. I understand that affirmation is necessary to keep you strong, and honor is vital to the soul of who you are. I will be your hiding place.

Sincerely,
Her

LOVE NOTE:

Anyone can offer him their body, but can they change his life and steady his course with their prayers and peace? Never get caught up in what society says we should become. Remember that women in scripture such as Abagail, Deborah, Esther, and Ruth, didn't have silicone, short dresses or 24"-inch extensions, yet they changed their part of the Kingdom with prayer, persistence, position, and even for some, prophecy.

There is a quiet power that comes with having a submitted heart that remains pure and intentional as it concerns our love for a man. We have the ear of God as his favorite daughters and what good father doesn't want to meet the need of a daughter who knows how to move in grace in such a clumsy world? What we carry in us can shift the entire atmosphere of our homes in any direction. Our prayers and peace for our men will allow them to hear the heart of God.

It does not make us voiceless, but rather a power that grows in silence, even in the most unfavorable situations. Our love and prayer softens their heart, as God changes their heart.

Confession

- Society does not dictate my posture, and
I am lead by examples of virtue and poise.

- Whatever area I do not feel confident in as
a woman in waiting, I will seek out others who have
information I need and I will glean

- Father, I will first be soft and submitted under
your care, that I may be in position to submit to my
husband.

- Because I am hidden in you and am learning to
trust you, I know you will only send the man I can
trust as well.

- I am not moved by biological clocks and
the expectations of others for my life. I am not
behind schedule, I am right on time and therefore I
will not pursue, who and what should pursue me.

PRAYER OF LOVE:

Father, thank you for being a father who looks out over your word to see that it be performed in the earth (*see* Jeremiah 1:12). Thank you for keeping your ear and your heart turned toward your daughters. God, we ask you now to keep our hearts pliable and without ill intention as we prepare for what you are preparing for us, in the way of a covering and husband.

Allow us to never harm your gift, by forgetting that he too will need patience and an ear just as we do. Posture us to be a hiding place when he is scared, and haunted by fears he has not found it easy to articulate to us for fear of being judged. Teach us to create an atmosphere of peace and hope in our home so that we won't be just another fight he has to work to win.

We know it is easy to love a man who is strong and solid. Place a grace inside of us that causes us to be sensitive enough to recognize when he needs our strength. We are learning each day what it means to truly be his help, and we are asking for you to be our instructor even when we think we know it all.

In Jesus' name, Amen.

Victory

"Wives, in the same way submit yourselves to your own husbands so that, if any of them do not believe in the word they may be won over without words by the behavior of their wives." (1 Peter 3:1 NIV)

The truth is that when our priests win, we win as well, because we are working on the same team. So the goal is to always be playing on the same side of the field as your partner. The term submission has become almost taboo. It is because some of the bad examples we saw of women, whether on movies or our reality simply taking what was given and being quiet. Those instances are not depictions of submission. Those are instances of becoming a doormat. Submission is simply a yielding of our own need to always be right and to be willing to be lead.

One of the greatest indicators of how a man will lead his home is by how is lead by the Lord and is submitted to someone more great than himself. When we are in a rush to be found, we will potentially overlook red flags in a man and convince ourselves that the red is really light pink instead. First, pay attention to how is takes instruction from his leader-whether it be a boss or his Pastor and see how he hears and moves by what the Lord gives him. If he can be lead with humility, he can lead with the same.

Before marriage, once you see that he is built to be a leader who will lead your home with integrity, submission to him prayerfully will come naturally. Because I witnessed my mother being taken advantage of as a child by my father I vowed to always be strong in marriage and not be walked on. That is out of order.

I am grateful that time, consecration and fully submitting to Lord years ago, broke that desire from me.

As long as your husband, is not asking you to do something that goes against your morals or value system, it is okay to simply be lead. It does not mean you do not have a voice; it simply says I do not need to raise mine to be heard over his. If the Lord trusts you with him then you are safe. If you trusted him enough to be your husband, allow him to also be your head. When you walk next to a decided man, he will fully understand that as you submit to him, and you both submit yourselves one to another under Christ, half the battles are already won...together.

Dear Future Husband,

The truth is, there were moments when I almost gave up on this journey. It wasn't because you aren't valuable and certainly not because you aren't worth it, but simply because my flesh would wonder if a flawed woman like me even deserved the man that I already know you to be. Just when I would begin to lose heart, I feel your prayers, and I'm reminded that you are awaiting our moment just as much as I am.

I find myself talking to you all the time. I speak Abba's word of grace over your life and the lives of anything connected to you. I can't wait until we lock eyes! I make it my daily assignment to touch the Father's hem on your behalf. This process has made me appreciate you even more and helps me stay clear of anything that isn't a reflection of God's love for me, because that is who you are.

In the times when I am afraid, I remember that the word decrees I don't have to be afraid when the love is divinely inspired and orchestrated. I know that you will never cause harm that can be avoided, because you will recognize that when I hurt, you too are pained. I am sorry for every tear you had to shed prior to me, but I am excited to know that love and commitment will be the softest of handkerchiefs against your cheeks.

Keep reaching in the dark for me. Soon it will be daylight, and you will find me there at daybreak.

Sincerely,
Her

Dear Future Husband,

Do my hands fit inside your palms? That is a question I have asked myself on more than one occasion. So, I excitedly anticipate you reaching down and interlocking your fingers with mines, for no other reason than just to be connected. After all, we spent years apart.

I look forward to the simple things, like smelling the side of your neck, and lying my curly ringlets against your chest to hear the strength of your beating heart. Next to my children, I have never covered anyone in the posture I have taken for you. I vow to be a watchman on the wall of your soul, keeping an eye on every happening that approaches your gates. You are precious, and because of your incomparable value, you are to be guarded and kept under the greatest of all care.

Who would let something as priceless and as pure hearted be tampered with. You are not just my priest, you are my whole and equal other half. You don't make me complete, because that would make you my idol, but you do make me grateful. For that reason, I vow to never take your presence for granted, to never dishonor our covenant, and to always be one of the consistent reasons that you thank God for daily.

This will never be a race. But I am ever so humbled

at the thoughts of our journey, the beauty that will come from our story, and the hope that others will find in our truth. Never stop searching for me. I am here.

Sincerely,
Her

Dear Future Husband,

I wonder what your laughter sounds like. The thought of seeing the light in your eyes, while you enjoy being tickled under your rib cage, makes me beam with joy. I don't just want you for your structure. I am anticipating the parts of you that are light and gentle. While in my presence, you are free to be everything the world may not make room for.

Your intellect and brilliance are not just welcomed but they are requested. I want to call you my very best friend, and mean every part of it. When all the world is a storm, I want to know there is safety underneath your covering. I just believe you will be able to speak to a storm and make it calm with your voice, the same as you will do with me when you tuck my curly locks behind my ears, and tell me everything is better than okay.

I want to offer you a love that is likened to a child——pure and without pretense, but mature enough to withstand turbulence and understand the idiosyncrasies of today while believing in the promises of a tomorrow.

You are not searching the heart of God foolishly for me, I know you are searching intentionally up and down every avenue of the Father for the one he is keeping tucked away for only you. Never worry, the seat in my heart is a place that only you will find rest. As the anticipation builds, so does my prayers over you, and my hope because of you. Keep searching his heart. I'm waiting.

Sincerely,
Her

Dear Future Husband,

Who would have known that the lips that pray for my children and speak your name into Heaven, will one day utter the words that will forever change our lives; "I do." I am excited to eat from the table set only by your heart. I desire to feast until I am satisfied. The thought of embracing you even for a moment sends my mind into a merry-go-round like motion, and I never want to stop spinning.

There is so much life to be lived, and even more territory to be taken together. This union won't just bless us, but it will create great echoes that will last longer than us. Although I am full of glee and bubbling over in anticipation, I remain sober and watchful over our promise. I stand guard in the spirit at the door which can only be accessed by you, through Father's permission. Thank you for being more magical than any once upon a wished-on star, more delightful than a playground full of children, and more insightful than a novel accredited with a noble peace——you are the prize.

Your love is the water and my hope in God for you is the manifested harvest. We have the seed, and we will never cease to sow. Everyday a new crop sprouts, and each year, another row of beautiful green Earth will spring forth between you and me. There is no drought in us, and no failure when we keep our love in the lap of almighty. Let's change the world.

Sincerely,
Her

Dear Future Husband,

I want to offer a level of honor and hope that you have never seen before. The kind of love that leaves freedom for truth and suffocates misunderstanding and irrational expectations. I want every strong place in me, to give refuge to every fragile place in you. I am grateful to know in my very being, that while you will be flawed, you will be worth every night spent on my face praying for your preparing.

I don't believe in fairytales, but I find bubbling excitement at the thought of skimming through every page of our life's journal and finding light even in the darkest of pages. Your love and protection will dig in the trenches of every untapped well and ends what seems to be a silent drought—you are water! I don't just desire your phone booth experience, because you are super–my man. I will love even the graying of your hair, because I understand that age brings wisdom and time offers resilience. As much as I wait for you, I dare not rush the process. I have seen what it is like to lose, and now I await our endless wins.

Sincerely,

Her

Confession

- Submission is not a curse or tool used to harm me

- No image in my childhood or past can cause me to mistreat who you send to cover me

- I am strong even when my voice is soft

- There is beauty in being lead, because I am the weaker vessel

- Lord, submission is your design and as I submit to my husband I am submitting unto you

LOVE NOTE:

If you aren't praying for him——willing to slobber unto Abba on his behalf, you aren't ready for him. There are dark things assigned to the lives of men as soon as their eyes open, because the enemy understands how valuable a properly positioned and whole man is. If you are only interested in his man parts and not his man struggles, then you will kill him while trying to caress him.

The next time you place your hand on the back of his neck, let it be to call down fire from Heaven, and not simply to rest between your thighs. Our men are perishing because we are selfish and self-seeking. We forget that even the strongest of them are fragile too.

We want his pockets and his pants but are you prepared to be his peace, and not just his piece? Do you have enough grace on your life and consecration in your walk to see the plan of the enemy coming for your man in the form of a woman two states away? Once you spot her, can you stop her before she even gets on the plane? Will he find hope in your lap or are you simply waiting for him to lay there so you can cut his hair, as Delilah did Samson? Be intentional in what you offer, and he will be intentional in how he plants his seed.

There is yet another chance for you to pen your heart. Take this time to write another letter to your future husband. Be candid, and unfiltered as you allow your heart to speak.

Dear Future Husband,

Sincerely,

Her

Truth

"Charm is deceptive, and beauty is fleeting; but a woman who fears the Lord is to be praised." (Proverbs 31:30 NIV)

WHAT MEN WANT

At the beginning of 2017, I took a poll via social media. A group of over thirty-five men recorded their thoughts on the qualities, features, and characteristics of women being wife material. They were asked to share two or three personal responses on what they deem to be wife material. My only instruction was that they did not have to give overly "churchy" answers, unless that was what they felt and meant. I did not change any part of their answers, as I wanted women to see the full truth in how they felt.

The findings were refreshing. I was not surprised that even when permitted to make mention of physical features, none of them did——not one. They have shared some of the things that the men felt were most valuable in a woman.

Mr. #1

"A strong prayer life, and a beautiful spirit. These are the two that are most attractive."

Mr. #2

"A woman who is intensely driven. She lives life, and life does not live her. She goes after what she wants and doesn't wait for things to happen. She must have an intellectual side, because looks can only keep the attention but so much. We have to be able to talk about more than pop culture.

My third attribute is style. Too many women only take pride in their appearance in certain places, for example in church, and work; yet, they look like "who shot John" all the other times. There was a time when women always had style, because, as my grandmother would say, "you never know who you are going to run into."

Mr. #3

"Honesty and being able to communicate outside of work or social media!"

Mr. #4

"The character of a woman is everything. Having and understanding ear and heart."

Mr. #5

"For me, her presence is important. Is she carrying peace, beauty, class, piercing wisdom, grace, and deep compassion?

Does she have high standards like how she dresses, how her house looks, what she accepts, and what she will not tolerate. Women with high standards generally elevate the life of their man! I'm blessed to have a wife who does that."

Mr. #6

"The ability to provide a safe place for me to rest, express myself, and lead along with me——doing so in a manner that preserves and builds my manhood. She must have the freedom to be affectionate and light-hearted, while keeping life simple.

To add a third thing, she has to want to be a wife——not just want to be married. I've noticed that women who are intentional about being a good wife strategically build their marriages, they give their best, and are expressive and passionate about loving, intimacy, and growing together.

Lord have mercy! That's the kind of wife husbands rush through traffic to get home to! Those kinds of women bring out the best in a man—their husband!"

Mr. #7

"Graciousness and kindness."

Mr. #8

"How she carries herself is important. Does she present herself as being a lady? It's so much more than just the way that she dresses.

Does she know how to hold a meaningful conversation? We need to talk about more than just what's happening on social media and reality T.V."

Mr. #9

So, as a man who's been married for 18 years and counting, here's what I discovered, I wanted and needed:

"A woman who's "interdependent". My wife can handle life when I'm not around. However, when I'm around there are things she needs me to do, and she will tell me. I don't have to be a Jedi to figure it all out. She is my cheerleader who knows how to cheer not just when we're winning, but encourages me when I'm down and it looks like it could be game over.

She is someone who sees me going to the bench to sit the rest of the game out and says, "nope you can't quit you can turn this thing around." Evidence of these traits should show up before walking down the aisle, and in my case, they did."

***

The women who witnessed the results were in amazement at what these men really needed. Most of the women thought men would say a round behind and a small waist, but there was such purity and absolute truth in what the men shared. It was easy to tell that they were not answering to gain brownie points, but rather to have a real voice that spoke louder than what society has painted a woman's value to be.

From this poll, we all understood that a man needs to genuinely see a woman's ability to bring value to his life, beyond her face or her curves. While the physical goes through changes over time, character is what keeps a person solid.

I have spent years talking to both men and women about what makes them motivated in love. What I have found habitually in men, is that honor and respect to them has the same impact as feeling beautiful and adored is to a woman. I have given counsel on more than a few occasions to women who did not understand why their intimate lives with their husbands had taken a turn for the worst, seemingly out of nowhere.

There are certain questions I ask to find the root, and almost always, the answer turned out to be that their husband's no longer felt honored or respected. Initially some of the women had worried that their husbands had been straying, and that was the reason for the change. The truth was simple——the sexiest woman may not be able to turn on a man whose spirit has been broken. A man with integrity won't just be ready to perform because there is a body in front of him.

How does the soul inside his wife's body cause him to feel? Are his dreams being heard? Does he feel his aspirations matter? Is he being undermined as it concerns the children? It is imperative that while preparing yourself to be a wife, that we learn how vital it is to a man to have an atmosphere conducive for him to dream and feel his work and his heart are equally as taken care of, as that of his wife.

Glory

"It is the glory of God to conceal a matter; to search out a matter is the glory of kings." (Proverbs 25:2 NIV)

We have all been guilty of having unrealistic expectations concerning the kind of man we want. Whether we want him to be extremely tall, dark versus light versus almond complexion, or with facial hair versus a baby face, and so on. That way of thinking has and will continue to cost many people the ability to be loved as they genuinely need, because they allow their preference to outshine what's been purposed.

Some media outlets, have fed us pictures of seemingly perfect men. It has made unrealistic expectations a hard beast to tame for the masses. The truth is that there is no perfect man, and even the most flawless man will seem flawed to someone. The goal is to commit to a man that has the core values, and most importantly, the qualities you need. He may not be tall,dark and handsome like you imagined since you married Barbie and Ken; maybe he is almond complexion and medium in height——but is he the best?

Society has already placed a plethora of expectations on the men that we know and love, and one of the worst things we can do is continue the trend when they come home. Create an atmosphere of peace. What you have not been taught, you can find answers to in prayer, or from talking to others who are successful in their relationship, in the areas you need some help in.

Never be afraid to take wise council from women who understand the value of relationships and can take you under their wing. The best time to start praying for and preparing for your future husband, is before he shows up.

LOVE NOTE:

One of the most powerful gifts we can give a man isn't sex, and not even a home cooked meal, but it is the ability to ask him what he needs and then pray for him until those things become his reality——also, to believe God to grant the silent desires that your beloved isn't able to share with you.

Another note for establishing a healthy bond with our future and for some, current husband, is understanding that they are not God, but they are a gift from him. A large group of women grew up playing with dolls, and playing house, thus causing them to see men as capable of saving us. In our eyes, they were the ones who would swoop down and carry us away from life's hardships, and we would kiss them just before they flew off to save the world. Do not allow unresolved issues to hold up the process of building your home.

As lovely as that sounds, that only works in the action movies. It is hugely key in our ability to have a balanced home, that we never put a man in the place of God. It is a sure way to be disappointed because they will fail a test they were unsure they were even taking.

No matter how amazing your husband will be, he can't make all life that existed before him disappear. Remember that he is not a genie. When we are finally whole in our single state, we will be ready to be the other whole side to a person. Utilize your singleness as a time of preparation. Use that time to heal, so that unrealistic desires don't take away opportunities for intimacy in the connection.

No matter how handy your man is, he will never be skilled

enough to fix you. Dig deep to deal with any unresolved, lingering hindrances that will prevent you from being his healthy and psychologically sound help-meet. The man who is being fashioned for us needs a woman who can add to his life and he to hers.

It is common for women to declare they are the Proverbs 31 woman over themselves, but she was a woman about building her home and being in position. Are you ready to build?

Confession

- No one can save me but you , Lord

- I desire the one you sent to love me- to cover me, but not to fix me-that is found in you.

- As I continue to find my purpose in you, I will see others properly and understand the role of my husband

- My husband is an extension of you, but he is not you. I will not break him, because he does not meet unrealistic expectations.
- Relationships do not make me whole. They simply add to who and what you have already said I am in you. Therefore, being single does not make me less valuable

- Thank you for continued healing and restoration. Your washing will continue to keep balance while I wait to be found, and even after marriage.

PRAYER OF LOVE:

Father, thank you for this time of preparation. Thank you Lord for instilling now in us what is necessary to love the son you are sending to us. Soften us in every area that may not allow us to have ears to hear even what he does not speak. Cause us to be awake and in position to be the heart of our homes. Teach us to offer our men a safe place for his dreams and his aspirations.

Even when we may not understand his desires, show us how to not question him to the point of negating his witty ideas because of our own lack of insight into them. We are to be their rib. Allow us to function as an extension of him, and not merely inspectors of their blueprints. We know they are to be the visionary of our homes, and we thank you for hearing our prayer as it concerns them. We look forward to being his glory and the brightest jewel in his crown.

In your son Jesus' name, Amen.

WOW, WE HAVE MADE IT TO THE END of this book, but it does not have to be the end of your journey to self-awareness, healing, and preparation.

I admonish future wives to honor your husbands, not just with your body, but with your words and what you pray over him. If he is praying, protecting, providing, and walking in purpose, then it is your responsibility to make sure he is dealt with in love and kindness.

He doesn't just want a meal and a feel. He needs a safe lap to lay his head in at the end of a distressing day. Be his "good thing," even when he still has no idea what that means. It doesn't make you a doormat; it makes you a wise woman who understands the importance of being his peace in a chaotic life. Whether you realize it or not, the heart of the wife sets the atmosphere of the home.

When he imparts his wisdom, she can receive the revelation, because she carries a part of his DNA within herself. That is why it is so important to stay sensitive to the needs of your man of God. He is looking to get a level of understanding and peace that should not be easily found in other people from you, his wife. His wife is his suitable help.

Take what you have learned here and expand on it. While you are waiting on him, work on yourself every day. You can never be too whole for as person. Seize the time of purposed singlehood. There is no such thing as being too whole, but there is such a thing as not being whole enough.

EARNEST HEART ACTIVITY

Take a moment to consider your future mate. This will take some self-reflection. Focus on what matters to you versus what your deal breakers are. This is a great exercise to help you put into perspective how realistic your personal desires are. Once you've pondered, write down the most important qualities in your future mate.

Write five of your top desirable qualities below.

_____

_____

_____

Now, here is where you jot down what your deal breakers.

_____

_____

_____

Did you answer anything differently than you

thought you would have? Once placed on paper, most people find that some of their previous deal breakers should not break deals after all. I implore your to be realistic and open to re-thinking things.

***

Thank you for bringing me along on this intimate walk with you. Keep writing your letters in your private journal, and watch how they evolve over your time of being hidden progresses. I match my faith to yours, that after you have been found pure, positioned, and empowered——when the Father sees fit to release it in the earth, you will be discovered.

EPILOGUE

"There is no fear in love. But perfect love drives out fear, because fear has to do with punishment. The one who fears is not made perfect in love." (1 John 4:18 NIV)

Constant acts of sexual impurity diminish the perfection of love. Sexual purity before marriage is a dying, but necessary decision. Even if you have fallen into sexual sin, it is not too late to get up and be restored. It is critical to give your husband the purest version of yourself. It was once said that women give sex to get love and men give love to get sex.

No matter how much you do for a man in bed, it will not make him cherish what is in your heart. If we are not careful, we can mistake a good lover for a great partner, and end up entrapped, because he can touch us in the right places. The way to avoid unnecessary traps is to simply stay away from ditches. Spend your single time pouring into yourself, and preparing your soul to be what is needed by another.

A man may not always say it, but in all the men I have counseled, the consensus was always the same——the idea that a woman kept her body in anticipation of marriage is viewed as a wonderful quality. My mother constantly told my friends, my female cousins, and myself that guys bed the party girls, and wed the women of substance.

I do believe that sex can ensnare women, because

we are groomed to love, and we convince ourselves that if we do enough, be enough, and for some, even sex enough, that we can make him see our value. Waiting also allows you to see a man's true character. It should be the desire of a woman to have a man pursue based on what you stand for, not what you are giving to him.

Any man interested in you must step into the spirit realm to unlock what's necessary to cover you, and not simply win you over in the bedroom. If he really commits to seeking God for what you need, he will find more than enough revelation to pursue, provide, and protect his wife. God has a plan. Do you trust it? Remember that you are valuable and your love, purity, passion, and purpose are more than enough for the right man.

***

Women who grow up in abusive environments, may at times find themselves battling in their mind more than with their mate. It is the small foxes that spoil the vine (Song of Solomon 2:15). This means that it may not always be something major that causes issues in your situations.

When you have learned to look at everyone who says they love you through the eyes of skepticism, you may find that same wound bleeding into your soul, hence your relationships. A heart that has been buried in garbage for so many years, will in fact assume everything around them stinks—if not delivered. The mental warfare that follows any type of abuse can completely asphyxiate the lines of healthy communication.

Be intentional with healing from past hurts, so that what should be healthy dialogue between our mate and us doesn't turn out ugly. Holding on to pain from someone who had no idea that love should come without pain is harmful. Brokenness makes it impossible to even take constructive criticism, and the gentlest nudge from our mate may be perceived as an attack.

The past can be poisonous to our present and future. The key to conquering this, is to commit to letting go of what was never meant to stay with us every day. Every day you must be intentional because the battle rages silently in our mind.

***

The task of transitioning from the head of your home, to the weaker vessel is usually daunting for women who have been single for any amount of years. There is however, a beauty that we are able to take on when we can release the reigns and realize that we no longer have to make every aspect of home work by ourselves.

It is more than vital to allow our man to lead the home as God leads him. Men were created to be needed and they will step up to the seat we set before them. Our need for them activates a superhero power, and they enjoy the ability to step in and bring order into the home——or any seemingly chaotic situation.

***

Even when you believe you have the answer, it is acceptable and wise to permit your priest the chance to save the day. You are his most treasured gift and showing him his value motivates him to keep you pretty and in your wifely position. You must learn to enjoy your power while maintaining your poise.

Be persistent in protecting the heart of your man, even if you are protecting it from yourself. The best time to guard your husband, is long before you meet him.

PRAYER OF LOVE:

Father, help us to understand that the power of our mouth is to speak purpose, praise, and pleasure to our present or future husbands. Help us to never demean or emasculate him. Teach us to be his biggest fan, greatest intercessor, and his safe place to fall.

Let us be surrounded by likeminded women who have our best interest at heart. Touch their hearts, so they can help us stay grounded and focused on what matters most in a healthy home. Strategically place us around wise counsel so that we can be successful—— even in the way we prepare for who and what is to come. Cause our expectations to be reasonable. Let them spew from a place of whole thinking. Cleanse them, that they may not be tainted with the residue of brokenness.

In Jesus' name, Amen.

Dear Forever Husband,

Thank you for your daily focus on your faith, purpose and family. I love the man that you were when we married, but daily I grow to adore you more for the man you diligently purpose your life to become. You have continued to be by far, one of my life's greatest supporters and the safety deposit box of so many of my heart's secrets. Your kisses are such a soft place to fall, and your arms are a strong tower of protection and rest for me.

I never knew the sound of someone else's laughter could provoke such a joy as yours has done even after all of this time. I honor your life and I am humbled and excited to unwrap the gift that is our journey each and every day.

Once upon a time, I was in search of a fairytale, and although we have indeed faced some fire breathing dragons, it is so fulfilling to see the fruit that remains. I honor you and as long as I have breath, I will stand against any lion ,bear and Philistine giant in the spirit on your behalf. I believe in you, and I am forever grateful for your life, love and this legacy. Thank you baby.

Sincerely,
Your Her

About the Author

Ebony Williams is an advocate for the broken hearted. Her heart for people and prophetic insight to the things of God, makes her an asset to the body of Christ, and the Kingdom of God. Chandler is a life coach, that specializes in the art of relationships and marriage.

She is an ordained preacher, licensed through the church and her life experiences to share the principles of Jesus Christ with hurting humanity. Through her healing retreats, many women and relationships are restored to a place of wholeness. Ebony resides in Metro-Atlanta with her husband and two children, where she continues to promote a love, life, and legacy for families worldwide.

Made in the USA
Columbia, SC
11 April 2018